MANIFESTING YOUR BEST LIFE

MANIFEST ANY THING IN YOUR LIFE, SUCH AS FINANCIAL ABUNDANCE, BETTER HEALTH, AND HAPPIER RELATIONSHIPS.

UMA NILAKANTAM

Made with ♥ on the Notion Press Platform
www.notionpress.com

This book is dedicated to my loving family and friends who have always supported me on my journey of self-discovery and personal growth. Your unwavering belief in me and your constant encouragement has been the driving force behind this work.

Your love, patience, and understanding have been a constant source of inspiration and motivation.

To my parents, thank you for instilling in me the values of hard work, perseverance, and self-belief. Your guidance and wisdom have been instrumental in shaping me into the person I am today.

And to all the readers who pick up this book, may you find the inspiration and tools you need to manifest your best life. May this work be a reminder that with the right mindset, dedication, and action, you can create the best life you truly desire.

With love and gratitude,

Uma Nilakantam

Contents

Foreword

In today's fast-paced world, it's easy to get caught up in the chaos and lose sight of what truly matters. We often find ourselves chasing after external goals and material possessions, believing that they will bring us happiness and fulfillment.

But what if I told you that the key to living your best life lies within you? What if I told you that you have the power to create the life you truly desire, by tapping into the limitless potential of your mind and spirit?

That's precisely what this book is about - manifesting your best life by harnessing the power of your thoughts, beliefs, and actions. It's a comprehensive guide that will take you on a journey of self-discovery and personal growth, helping you to unleash your full potential and live a life of purpose and abundance.

Drawing upon the latest research in psychology, neuroscience, and spirituality, this book offers a unique blend of practical tools and insightful wisdom. Whether you're looking to enhance your career, improve your relationships, or simply find more joy and meaning in your everyday life, this book has something to offer.

But more than that, this book is a testament to the power of the human spirit. It's a reminder that no matter what challenges we may face, we have the strength and resilience to overcome them and create a life of our dreams. So, I invite you to dive into this book with an open mind and an open heart, and let it guide you on your path to manifesting your best life.

Warmly,
Uma Nilakantam

Preface

Welcome to "**Manifesting Your Best Life**," a guidebook for those seeking to create a life of purpose, joy, and abundance. This book is a culmination of my own personal journey of self-discovery and growth, as well as the insights and lessons I've learned from working with countless clients over the years.

At the heart of this book is the belief that we all have the power to manifest the life we desire, by harnessing the power of our thoughts, beliefs, and actions. It's a philosophy that has been echoed throughout history by spiritual leaders, philosophers, and scientists alike - that a mind is a powerful tool, capable of shaping our reality.

But while the concept of manifesting is not new, the science behind it is only beginning to emerge. In this book, I've drawn upon the latest research in psychology, neuroscience, and spirituality to offer a comprehensive framework for manifesting your best life.

The book sets the foundation, exploring the concept of manifesting and the power of the mind. Delves into the practical tools and techniques for manifesting, including visualization, affirmations, and gratitude practices. It also offers guidance on overcoming common obstacles and challenges that may arise on the path to manifesting your best life.

But more than just a practical guide, this book is an invitation to embark on a journey of self-discovery and personal growth. It's a call to awaken the inner wisdom and potential that lies within each of us and to step into our power as creators of our own destiny.

I hope that this book will inspire and guide you on your path to manifesting your best life and that it will be a source of support and encouragement as you navigate the ups and downs of life. May it be a reminder that you have within you the power to create the life of your dreams.

With love and gratitude,
Uma Nilakantam

Acknowledgements

Writing this book has been a journey of self-discovery, growth, and transformation, and I couldn't have done it without the support and encouragement of so many people. I would like to express my heartfelt gratitude to:

My family and friends, for their unwavering belief in me and their constant support throughout this journey.

My clients, have entrusted me with their stories and allowed me to witness their incredible transformations.

My editor, for her insightful feedback, patience, and guidance throughout the writing process.

My agent, for her belief in this book and her unwavering support throughout the publishing process.

The team at the publishing house, for their hard work and dedication in bringing this book to life.

And to all the spiritual leaders, philosophers, scientists, and writers who have inspired me along the way thank you for sharing your wisdom and insights.

Finally, I would like to express my deepest gratitude to the readers of this book. It is my hope that this work will inspire and guide you on your journey to manifesting your best life, and that it will be a source of support and encouragement as you navigate the ups and downs of life.

With love and gratitude,

Uma Nilakantam

Prologue

Have you ever felt like there was more to life than what you're currently experiencing? Like there a deeper purpose or calling waiting to be discovered?

If you're reading this book, chances are you're looking to tap into that deeper sense of purpose and create a life that truly fulfills you. Perhaps you're feeling stuck in your career, struggling in your relationships, or simply feeling unfulfilled and uncertain about your future.

But the good news is that you're not alone. We all experience moments of doubt, fear, and uncertainty, and we all have the capacity to overcome them and create the life of our dreams.

The key to unlocking this potential lies within you - specifically, in your thoughts, beliefs, and actions. By harnessing the power of your mind and spirit, you can manifest the life you truly desire, and live a life of purpose, joy, and abundance.

This book is a guidebook for that journey. It's a comprehensive roadmap for those seeking to tap into their inner wisdom and potential and create the life of their dreams. It draws upon the latest research in psychology, neuroscience, and spirituality, and offers a unique blend of practical tools and insightful wisdom.

But more than that, this book is an invitation to embark on a journey of self-discovery and personal growth. It's a call to awaken the inner wisdom and potential that lies within each of us and to step into our power as creators of our own destiny.

So, if you're ready to embark on this journey, I invite you to dive into this book with an open mind and an open heart. May it be a source of inspiration, guidance, and support as you manifest your best life.

With love and gratitude,

Uma Nilakantam

Who Is Uma Nilakantam?

Uma Nilakantam is a renowned **manifestation coach**, **Ho'oponopono healer**, and **Law of Attraction coach** with 8 years of experience in the field. She is also an author, speaker, and social media specialist who has helped countless individuals and businesses worldwide to achieve their goals and live fulfilling lives.

As a manifestation coach, Uma helps people tap into the power of their thoughts and emotions to attract positive outcomes and manifest their dreams into reality. Her expertise in the Ho'oponopono healing practice further helps individuals to release negative emotions, limiting beliefs, and past traumas that might be blocking their progress.

Uma is also an experienced Law of Attraction coach, helping individuals to understand and implement the powerful law that governs the universe. Through one-on-one coaching sessions, corporate events, and workshops, Uma provides customized guidance and practical tools to help people attract abundance, success, and happiness into their lives. In addition to her coaching and healing services,

Uma and her team also provide social media management services, including Instagram, Facebook, and YouTube channel management. They have helped numerous celebrities, influencers, and coaches to build a strong online presence and connect with their followers. With Uma's guidance and support, you can get exactly what you need to make life great. Whether you're looking to achieve your personal or professional goals,

Uma's coaching and healing services can help you unlock your full potential and live a fulfilling life. Contact Uma and her team today to learn more about how they can help you manifest your dreams and reach new heights of success.

CHAPTER ONE

Introduction

"Your thoughts create your reality. Manifest your dreams by thinking positively, believing wholeheartedly, and taking inspired action." - Uma Nilakantam

Briefly explain what manifestation is and how it works

Manifestation is the idea that we can create our reality through the power of our thoughts and beliefs. It is based on the premise that we are all connected to a universal energy that responds to our thoughts and feelings, and that we can use this energy to attract our desired outcomes into our lives.

At its core, manifestation is about aligning our thoughts, emotions, and actions with our goals and intentions. By focusing our attention on what we want, rather than what we don't want, we can shift our perception of the world around us and create new opportunities for growth and success.

The process of manifestation typically involves several key steps. First, we must identify our desired outcome and set a clear intention for what we want to manifest. This could be anything from financial abundance to better health to a more fulfilling relationship.

Once we have set our intention, we must then visualize ourselves already having achieved our desired outcome. This involves using our imagination to create a vivid mental picture of what it would look, feel, and sound like to have our goal already manifested in our lives. This step is important because it helps create a strong emotional connection to our goal and reinforces our belief that achieving is possible.

The next step in the manifestation process is to take inspired action toward our goal. This could involve anything from learning new skills to networking with others who can help us achieve our goal to taking small steps every day towards our desired outcome. By taking action, we demonstrate our commitment to our goal and signal to the universe that we are ready and willing to receive the resources, opportunities, and support we need to make it a reality.

Finally, manifestation also involves cultivating a positive mindset and maintaining a high level of energy and enthusiasm for our goal. This could involve practicing gratitude, affirmations, or visualization techniques regularly to help reinforce our belief in our ability to manifest our desires.

While the specifics of manifestation techniques may vary, the underlying principle remains the same: we have the power to creour reality through the power of our thoughts and beliefs. By aligning our thoughts, emotions, and actions with our goals and intentions, we can tap into the universal energy that surrounds us and bring our desires into physical reality.

Of course, it's worth noting that manifestation is not a magic solution to all of life's problems. It requires effort, patience, and persistence to achieve our goals, and there will inevitably be setbacks and obstacles along the way. However, by cultivating a positive mindset and focusing our attention on what we want, we can create a more fulfilling and satisfying life for ourselves, and tap into the limitless potential that exists within us all.

Importance of having a clear intention, a positive mindset, and taking action toward your goals

Clear intention:

Having a clear intention is essential for manifesting any desire because it helps to focus your mind and energy toward achieving your goal. When you have a clear intention, you have a clear picture of what you want to manifest, and this clarity helps you to take the necessary actions to make your desire a reality.

Here are some reasons why having a clear intention is important:

1. **Focus:** Having a clear intention helps you to focus your thoughts and energy toward your goal. This focus helps you to eliminate distractions and concentrate on what you want to manifest.

2. **Motivation:** When you have a clear intention, you are more motivated to take action toward your goal. Your intention acts as a driving force that pushes you towards achieving your desire.
3. **Clarity:** A clear intention gives you a clear understanding of what you want to manifest, and this clarity helps you to make better decisions and take more effective actions toward your goal.
4. **Visualization:** When you have a clear intention, it is easier to visualize yourself achieving your Visualizationlization is a powerful tool for manifesting because it helps to create a mental image of what you want to achieve.
5. **Alignment:** When you have a clear intention, you are more aligned with the universe and the energy around you. This alignment helps to attract the right people, opportunities, and resources toward you, which can help you to manifest your desire more easily.

Overall, having a clear intention is essential for manifesting any desire. It helps you to focus your thoughts and energy toward your goal, motivates you to take action, gives you clarity and visualization, and aligns you with the energy around you.

Importance of having a positive mindset towards your goals

Having a positive mindset is crucial for manifesting any desire because our thoughts and beliefs have a powerful impact on our actions, emotions, and ultimately, our outcomes. A positive mindset helps you to cultivate a more optimistic and empowering perspective, which can influence how you approach challenges, opportunities, and setbacks on your journey toward manifesting your desires. Here are some reasons why having a positive mindset is important:

1. **Attracts positivity:** A positive mindset attracts positivity and abundance into your life. When you focus on positive thoughts and emotions, you emit a high frequency of energy that can attract positive people, opportunities, and experiences toward you.
2. **Boosts confidence:** A positive mindset can boost your confidence and self-belief, which is essential for taking bold actions and pursuing your goals. When you believe in yourself and your ability to manifest your

desires, you are more likely to take action toward them.

3. **Reduces stress:** A positive mindset can reduce stress and anxiety, which can inhibit your ability to focus on your desires and take inspired action. By focusing on positive thoughts and emotions, you can reduce stress and increase your mental and emotional resilience.
4. **Improves creativity:** A positive mindset can improve your creativity and problem-solving skills, which are essential for finding innovative solutions to challenges that may arise during your manifestation journey.
5. **Increases gratitude:** A positive mindset can increase your sense of gratitude and appreciation for the present moment and the blessings in your life. This gratitude can create a positive cycle of abundance and attract even more positivity and abundance toward you.

Overall, having a positive mindset is essential for manifesting any desire. It helps you to attract positivity, boost your confidence, reduce stress, improve creativity, and increase gratitude. By cultivating a positive mindset, you can enhance your ability to manifest your desires and create a more fulfilling and abundant life.

Importance of taking action toward your goals

Taking action toward your goals is a crucial component of manifestation because manifestation is not simply about wishing for something to happen; it also requires active participation and effort from you. Here are some reasons why taking action is important:

1. **Manifestation is a co-creative process:** Manifestation is a co-creative process that involves both you and the universe. While you need to set your intentions and visualize your desires clearly, you must also take inspired action toward them. Action is a crucial component of the manifestation process because it shows the universe that you are committed to achieving your desires.
2. **Builds momentum:** Taking action towards your goals builds momentum and helps you to stay motivated and focused. When you take small steps towards your desires every day, you create a sense of progress and accomplishment that can fuel your manifestation journey.
3. **Attracts opportunities:** Taking action toward your goals can attract new opportunities and resources to you. By putting yourself out there and

taking bold steps towards your desires, you open yourself up to new possibilities and connections that can help you to manifest your desires more easily.

4. **Creates a sense of empowerment:** Taking action toward your goals can create a sense of empowerment and self-confidence. When you take ownership of your manifestation journey and take inspired action toward your desires, you build a stronger sense of self-efficacy and belief in your ability to create the life you want.
5. **Amplifies manifestation:** Taking action amplifies the manifestation process by creating a positive feedback loop between your thoughts, emotions, and actions. When you take action toward your desires, you create more positive thoughts and emotions that can attract even more positivity and abundance toward you.

Overall, taking action toward your goals is an essential component of the manifestation process. It builds momentum, attracts opportunities, creates a sense of empowerment, and amplifies manifestation. By taking inspired action toward your desires, you can co-create the life you want and achieve your goals with greater ease and joy.

Conclusion:

Having a clear intention, a positive mindset, and taking action towards your goals is important for several reasons:

1. **Clarity of Purpose:** Having a clear intention helps you focus on what you want to achieve and guides you toward your goals. When you have a clear understanding of your objectives, you can make informed decisions and take effective actions toward their accomplishment.
2. **Positive Mindset:** A positive mindset is crucial in helping you overcome challenges and obstacles along the way. When you have a positive outlook, you are more likely to see opportunities rather than problems and have the resilience to keep going even when things get tough.
3. **Taking Action:** Taking action is the most critical step in achieving your goals. No matter how positive your mindset or clear your intention is unless you take action, your goals will remain just that - goals. By taking action, you bring your goals to life and increase your chances of success.

In conclusion, having a clear intention, a positive mindset, and taking action toward your goals are all essential elements in achieving your desired outcomes. By focusing on these three areas, you can increase your chances of success and live a more fulfilling life.

Some positive mindset affirmations that you may find helpful:

1. *I am capable of achieving great things.*
2. *I choose to focus on the positive in all situations.*
3. *I am worthy of love, success, and happiness.*
4. *I am grateful for all the blessings in my life.*
5. *I trust the universe to guide me toward my highest good.*
6. *I have the power to create the life I desire.*
7. *I am constantly growing and evolving as a person.*
8. *I am confident in my abilities and believe in myself.*
9. *I am surrounded by abundance and prosperity.*
10. *I am capable of overcoming any challenges that come my way.*

Remember that affirmations are most effective when you repeat them regularly and truly believe in their power to shape your thoughts and emotions. With consistent practice, you can cultivate a positive and empowering mindset that will help you achieve your goals and lead a fulfilling life.

Briefly explain what manifestation is and how it works

Manifestation is the idea that you can bring your desires and goals to reality through the power of your thoughts, beliefs, and emotions. It's based on the concept that our thoughts and beliefs have a direct impact on the events and experiences in our lives.

The process of manifestation typically involves focusing your attention on what you want to manifest, visualizing yourself already having it, and aligning your thoughts, beliefs, and emotions with the experience of having it. This can involve practices such as affirmations, visualization, and gratitude.

Proponents of manifestation believe that the universe responds to your thoughts and feelings and that by focusing on positive, high-frequency thoughts and emotions, you can attract positive experiences and outcomes into your life. On the other hand, if you focus on negative thoughts and feelings, you may attract negative experiences.

While manifestation is not a scientifically proven, many people find that incorporating manifestation techniques into their lives can help them clarify their goals, build confidence, and bring more joy and abundance into their lives. However, manifestation should not be seen as a substitute for taking action toward your goals, but rather as a way to align your thoughts and emotions with what you want to achieve.

A manifestation is a powerful tool, but not a magic solution - it requires effort and persistence

Yes, that's correct. The concept of manifestation involves focusing your thoughts, beliefs, and emotions towards a desired outcome or goal, with the belief that you can bring it into reality. However, manifestation is not a one-time process, but rather a continuous and ongoing effort. It requires consistent focus, effort, and persistence to align your thoughts, beliefs, and actions with your desired outcome, and to make it a reality. Simply visualizing and wishing for something is not enough, as you must also take action toward achieving your goal. Therefore, manifestation requires a combination of both mental effort and physical effort to be truly effective.

A manifestation is indeed a powerful tool that can help you achieve your goals and bring positive changes into your life. However, it is important to understand that manifestation is not a magic solution that will magically make everything you want to come to you with no effort on your part. It requires effort, persistence, and a strong belief in yourself and your abilities.

Manifestation works by aligning your thoughts, beliefs, and emotions with what you want to achieve. You must focus on what you want, visualize it, and feel the emotions associated with having it as if it has already happened. This creates a powerful energy that attracts similar energies and brings your desires closer to you.

However, manifestation is not a one-time process. It requires consistent effort and a commitment to your goals. You must be persistent in your visualization and affirmations, and you must take action toward your goals. This means that you need to put in the work, take steps toward your goals, and overcome any obstacles that may arise along the way.

In conclusion, manifestation is a powerful tool, but it is not a magic solution. It requires effort, persistence, and a strong belief in yourself and your abilities. If you are willing to put in the work, manifestation can help you bring your desires to life.

CHAPTER TWO

Manifesting Financial Abundance

Discuss the role of our thoughts and beliefs in shaping our financial reality

Our thoughts and beliefs play a significant role in shaping our financial reality. They can have a powerful influence on our behaviors, decisions, and actions related to money, which in turn impact our financial outcomes. Here are some ways in which thoughts and beliefs shape our financial reality:

1. **Attitudes towards money:** Our beliefs about money can influence how we view and prioritize it in our lives. If someone believes that money is the root of all evil, they may avoid or be indifferent to financial opportunities, leading to lower financial security. On the other hand, if someone views money as a tool for achieving their goals, they may be more proactive in pursuing financial stability and growth.
2. **Money mindset:** Our thoughts and beliefs about money can shape our money mindset, which can either limit or expand our financial possibilities. If someone believes that they are not good with money or will never be able to save, they may avoid taking control of their finances, leading to continued financial struggles. However, if someone has a growth mindset and believes they can improve their financial situation, they may be more open to learning and taking action to improve their finances.
3. **Decision-making:** Our thoughts and beliefs can also impact the financial decisions we make. For example, if someone believes that taking financial risks is always a bad idea, they may avoid investment

opportunities that could potentially lead to financial growth. On the other hand, if someone believes in taking calculated risks, they may be more willing to explore and pursue investment opportunities.

4. **Habits and behavior:** Our thoughts and beliefs can also shape our financial habits and behavior. If someone believes that spending more than they earn is acceptable, they may engage in excessive spending, leading to financial difficulties. However, if someone believes in living within their means and saving for the future, they may be more likely to adopt responsible spending habits and build financial stability.

In conclusion, our thoughts and beliefs play a critical role in shaping our financial reality. It is essential to be aware of and challenge limiting beliefs, and cultivate a positive and growth-oriented mindset towards money to achieve financial stability and growth.

Tips and techniques for shifting limiting beliefs and cultivating a prosperity mindset

What are the Limiting Beliefs?

Limiting beliefs are beliefs that hold us back and prevent us from reaching our full potential.

Limiting beliefs are beliefs that hold us back and prevent us from reaching our full potential. They can be negative and self-defeating thoughts that limit our abilities, opportunities, and outcomes. Examples of limiting beliefs include "I'm not good enough," "I can never succeed," or "Money is the root of all evil." These beliefs can be deeply ingrained and may have been developed from past experiences or societal messages.

Here are some steps to identify your limiting beliefs:

1. **Pay attention to your thoughts:** Observe your thoughts and feelings and be mindful of the negative and self-defeating thoughts that come up regularly.
2. **Identify patterns:** Look for patterns in your thoughts and beliefs. Are there certain beliefs that come up frequently and hold you back from

taking action?

3. **Reflect on your past experiences:** Consider your past experiences and the messages you received growing up. Do you have beliefs about yourself or the world that are limiting and no longer serve you?
4. **Seek outside perspectives:** Talk to trusted friends and family members and ask for their perspectives on your beliefs and limitations. They may be able to offer a different point of view and help you identify limiting beliefs that you have not yet recognized.
5. **Write it down:** Write down your limiting beliefs and reflect on how they impact your life and hold you back. By writing them down, you can gain a clearer understanding of their impact and start the process of challenging and reframing them.

By being mindful of your thoughts and beliefs and taking the steps to identify limiting beliefs, you can start to challenge and change them, leading to greater personal and financial growth and success.

They can be negative and self-defeating thoughts that limit our abilities, opportunities, and outcomes. Some common limiting beliefs include:

1. *"I am not good with money."*
2. *"I will never be able to save."*
3. *"I am not smart enough to invest."*
4. *"I can never make enough money."*
5. *"I am not worthy of financial success."*

These limiting beliefs can be deeply ingrained and may have been developed from past experiences or societal messages. However, they can also be challenged and changed with effort and dedication. By recognizing and reframing limiting beliefs, individuals can shift their perspective and adopt a more positive and growth-oriented mindset, leading to greater financial stability and growth.

How to Shift those limiting beliefs?

Shifting limiting beliefs and cultivating a prosperous mindset can be a challenge, but with dedication and effort, it can lead to greater financial stability and growth. Here are some tips and techniques for shifting limiting beliefs and cultivating a prosperity mindset:

1. **Awareness:** The first step in shifting limiting beliefs is to become aware of them. Pay attention to the thoughts and beliefs that hold you back and prevent you from reaching your financial goals. Write them down and reflect on their impact on your financial situation.
2. **Reframe negative thoughts:** Once you have identified limiting beliefs, it's essential to reframe them into positive, empowering thoughts. For example, instead of thinking "I can never save money," try reframing it to "I am learning to manage my finances and save for the future."
3. **Surround yourself with positive influences:** Seek out people and resources that support and encourage your financial goals. Surround yourself with people who have a positive and growth-oriented mindset toward money and seek out books, podcasts, and online resources that provide financial education and inspiration.
4. **Practice gratitude:** Cultivate a habit of gratitude and focus on what you have instead of what you lack. Appreciating what you have can shift your perspective from scarcity to abundance and help you develop a more positive and growth-oriented mindset toward money.
5. **Visualization:** Visualize yourself having financial stability and abundance. See yourself achieving your financial goals and experiencing the joy and freedom that come with financial prosperity. Regularly visualize your desired financial reality to help make it a reality.
6. **Take action:** Taking consistent and focused action towards your financial goals is essential in shifting limiting beliefs and cultivating a prosperous mindset. Set specific and achievable financial goals, develop a budget, seek out investment opportunities, and take steps toward financial stability and growth.

In *conclusion*, shifting limiting beliefs and cultivating a prosperous mindset takes time, effort, and consistent action. By being aware of limiting beliefs, reframing negative thoughts, surrounding yourself with positive influences, practicing gratitude, visualizing your desired financial reality, and taking focused action, you can move towards financial stability and growth.

Practical strategies for increasing income, reducing debt, and building wealth

Here are some practical strategies for increasing income, reducing debt, and building wealth:

Increasing Income:

Here are some practical strategies for increasing income:

1. Look for ways to increase your salary or negotiate for a raise at work. This can be done by taking on additional responsibilities, developing new skills, or demonstrating your value to the company.
2. Start a side hustle or freelance gig. This can be anything from offering your services as a consultant to starting an e-commerce business.
3. Rent out a room or space in your home on a platform like Airbnb.
4. Sell items you no longer need or want. This can include clothes, electronics, or other items you no longer use.
5. Participate in paid surveys or sign up for focus groups. Many market research companies are willing to pay for your opinions.
6. Offer your skills as a tutor or coach in a subject you're knowledgeable in.
7. Start a small business, such as a pet-sitting or dog-walking service.
8. Invest in real estates, such as rental properties.
9. Participate in the gig economy, such as driving for a ride-sharing service or delivering food.

Remember that the key to increasing your income is finding a way to monetize your skills, knowledge, or resources. It may take some time and effort, but the payoff can be significant.

Here are some affirmations for increasing income that you can use to focus your mind on abundance and attract more financial prosperity into your life:

1. *I am a magnet for abundance and prosperity.*
2. *I am grateful for the increasing income that flows into my life.*
3. *My income is constantly increasing and expanding.*
4. *I deserve to be financially prosperous and abundant.*
5. *I am open to new opportunities and channels for increasing my income.*
6. *The universe is conspiring in my favor to bring me greater financial abundance.*
7. *I am worthy of receiving unlimited abundance and prosperity.*

8. *I trust that my financial situation is improving every day.*
9. *I am attracting opportunities that will bring me financial freedom and security.*
10. *Money flows to me easily and effortlessly, and I am grateful for this abundance.*

Remember to repeat these affirmations daily with a sense of belief and positivity, and visualize yourself already having the abundance and prosperity you desire. By aligning your thoughts and emotions with the frequency of abundance, you can attract more financial prosperity into your life.

Reducing Debt:

Here are some practical strategies for reducing debt:

1. Make a budget and stick to it. This will help you keep track of your spending and identify areas where you can cut back.
2. Prioritize paying off high-interest debt first, such as credit card balances. This will help you save money on interest charges and reduce your debt more quickly.
3. Consider debt consolidation or a debt management plan. This can help simplify your debt repayment process and potentially reduce your interest rates.
4. Cut back on non-essential expenses, such as eating out or subscription services. This can free up money to put towards paying off debt.
5. Increase your income by taking on a side job or selling unused items. This can help you pay off debt faster.
6. Avoid taking on new debt while you're working to pay off existing debt.
7. Make more than the minimum payment on your debt each month. This can help reduce the amount of interest you pay over time.
8. Negotiate with your creditors. You may be able to lower your interest rates or negotiate a payment plan that works better for you.

Remember that reducing debt takes time and discipline, but the payoff can be significant. It's important to stay focused and motivated and to remember that every little bit helps.

Here are some affirmations for reducing debt that you can use to focus your mind on financial freedom and attract more abundance into your life:

1. *I am free from the burden of debt and I am financially abundant.*
2. *I am grateful for the abundance that is flowing into my life and reducing my debt.*
3. *I release all limiting beliefs and patterns around debt and welcome financial freedom.*
4. *I am worthy of a debt-free life and financial abundance.*
5. *I am taking positive steps every day to reduce my debt and achieve financial freedom.*
6. *I trust that the universe is guiding me toward greater financial stability and abundance.*
7. *I am attracting abundance and prosperity into my life, which is reducing my debt.*
8. *I am grateful for the abundance that is allowing me to pay off my debt easily and effortlessly.*
9. *I am open to receiving new opportunities and channels for reducing my debt and achieving financial freedom.*
10. *I trust that the universe is conspiring in my favor to help me reduce my debt and achieve financial abundance.*

Remember to repeat these affirmations daily with a sense of belief and positivity, and visualize yourself already living a debt-free life with financial freedom and abundance. By aligning your thoughts and emotions with the frequency of financial freedom, you can attract more abundance into your life and reduce your debt with greater ease and joy.

Building Wealth:

Here are some practical strategies for building wealth:

1. Start by contributing to a retirement account, such as a 401(k) or IRA. This will help you take advantage of compound interest and tax benefits, and can set you on the path to financial independence.
2. Invest in a diversified portfolio of low-cost index funds or exchange-traded funds (ETFs). This can help you maximize your returns and reduce the risk associated with investing.

3. Pay off high-interest debt to reduce the amount of interest you pay over time. This can help free up money to put towards saving and investing.
4. Increase your income by taking on a side job or freelance gig. This can help you build wealth faster by giving you more money to invest.
5. Live below your means and avoid lifestyle inflation. This can help you save more money and reduce your debt, which will in turn help you build wealth faster.
6. Consider buying rental properties. This can provide a steady source of passive income and build wealth over time.
7. Start a small business. This can help you earn additional income and potentially grow your wealth faster.
8. Make smart spending decisions. Look for ways to save money on everyday expenses, and consider your long-term financial goals when making large purchases.

Remember that building wealth takes time and patience, but by setting achievable goals and staying disciplined, you can set yourself on the path to financial freedom. It's also important to consult with a financial advisor to make sure you're on the right track and to get personalized advice.

Here are some affirmations for building wealth that you can use to focus your mind on abundance and attract more financial prosperity into your life:

1. *I am a magnet for wealth and abundance, and I attract it effortlessly into my life.*
2. *I am worthy of building wealth and creating financial freedom for myself and my loved ones.*
3. *I trust that the universe is guiding me toward greater wealth and prosperity.*
4. *I am grateful for the wealth that is flowing into my life every day, and I use it wisely to create a better life for myself and those around me.*
5. *I am open to new opportunities and channels for building wealth and creating financial abundance.*
6. *I am constantly learning and growing in my ability to build wealth and create financial freedom.*
7. *I am attracting abundance and prosperity into my life, which is allowing me to build wealth with ease and joy.*
8. *I am worthy of receiving unlimited wealth and abundance, and I embrace this abundance with gratitude and joy.*

9. *I trust that my wealth is growing every day, and I am taking inspired action toward my financial goals.*
10. *I am grateful for the abundance and wealth that is already present in my life, and I attract even more of it with positive thoughts and emotions.*

Remember to repeat these affirmations daily with a sense of belief and positivity, and visualize yourself already living a wealthy and abundant life. By aligning your thoughts and emotions with the frequency of wealth and abundance, you can attract more financial prosperity into your life and create the financial freedom and abundance you desire.

Note that these strategies may not be suitable for everyone and it is important to do your own research and consult a financial advisor before making any investment decisions.

"Whatever the mind can conceive and believe, it can achieve." - Napoleon Hill

CHAPTER THREE

Manifesting Better Health

Discuss the connection between our thoughts and feelings and our physical health

The connection between our thoughts, feelings, and physical health is well-established and has been the subject of numerous studies and research in the fields of psychology, neuroscience, and medicine.

The human body and mind are interconnected and interdependent. Our thoughts, emotions, and mental state can have a significant impact on our physical health and well-being.

The connection between our thoughts, feelings, and physical health is complex and bidirectional. Our thoughts and emotions can have a profound impact on our physical health, and similarly, physical health problems can also affect our thoughts and emotions.

When we experience negative emotions such as stress, anxiety, or depression, our bodies respond with a release of stress hormones like cortisol and adrenaline. This fight-or-flight response can cause physical symptoms such as headaches, muscle tension, and an elevated heart rate. Chronic stress can also weaken the immune system, increase the risk of cardiovascular disease, and disrupt sleep patterns, among other negative effects on physical health.

On the other hand, positive thoughts and emotions such as happiness, gratitude, and compassion can have a positive impact on physical health. Engaging in activities that promote positive emotions and reduce stress, such as mindfulness meditation, yoga, and exercise, can help regulate the stress response and reduce inflammation, leading to improved physical health.

It's also important to note that physical health problems can affect our thoughts and emotions. Chronic pain, for example, can lead to depression and anxiety, while poor sleep can result in a decreased ability to regulate emotions.

In summary, our thoughts and emotions play a critical role in our physical health and well-being, and it's important to cultivate positive thoughts and emotions and manage stress effectively to maintain optimal health.

Tips and techniques for reducing stress and improving physical and emotional well-being

There are several ways to reduce stress and improve physical and emotional well-being:

1. **Exercise:** Regular exercise is one of the best ways to reduce stress and improve physical and emotional well-being. Exercise releases endorphins which are natural mood boosters and can help to reduce anxiety and depression. Aim for at least 30 minutes of moderate physical activity every day.
2. **Meditation and mindfulness:** Meditation and mindfulness practices help to calm the mind and reduce stress. Try to set aside a few minutes each day to meditate, practice deep breathing, or simply be present at the moment.
3. **Good sleep habits:** Getting enough sleep is essential for both physical and emotional well-being. Establish a bedtime routine, avoid screens for at least an hour before bedtime, and create a relaxing sleep environment.
4. **Healthy eating:** A balanced diet is important for physical and emotional well-being. Eat plenty of fruits and vegetables, whole grains, and lean proteins, and limit your intake of sugar, caffeine, and alcohol.
5. **Connect with others:** Spending time with loved ones, joining a club or organization, or volunteering can help reduce stress and improve your emotional well-being.
6. **Seek support:** Talking to a therapist or counselor can be a helpful way to manage stress and improve emotional well-being.
7. **Take breaks:** Taking regular breaks throughout the day can help reduce stress and improve physical and emotional well-being. Go for a walk, read a book, or simply take a few deep breaths.

Remember, everyone is different and what works for one person may not work for another. It's important to find what works best for you and make self-care a regular part of your routine.

Here are some affirmations for reducing the stress that you can use to calm your mind and attract more peace and relaxation into your life:

1. *I release all tension and stress from my body, and I am filled with peace and calm.*
2. *I am in control of my thoughts and emotions, and I choose to focus on peace and relaxation.*
3. *I trust that everything is working out for my highest good, and there is no need to worry or stress.*
4. *I am surrounded by love and support, and I allow this love to ease my stress and anxiety.*
5. *I am grateful for this moment of calm and relaxation, and I allow myself to fully embrace it.*
6. *I am breathing deeply and calmly, and I am filled with a sense of inner peace and tranquility.*
7. *I am capable of handling any challenges that come my way, and I trust in my ability to overcome stress and anxiety.*
8. *I am taking care of myself and my needs, and I prioritize my well-being and relaxation.*
9. *I am releasing all negative thoughts and emotions, and I am filling my mind with positive thoughts and emotions that promote peace and calm.*
10. *I am creating a life of peace and relaxation, and I am attracting people and experiences that support this peaceful lifestyle.*

Remember to repeat these affirmations daily with a sense of belief and positivity, and visualize yourself already living a stress-free life filled with peace and relaxation. By aligning your thoughts and emotions with the frequency of peace and calm, you can attract more relaxation and tranquility into your life and reduce stress and anxiety with greater ease and joy.

Practical strategies for making healthy lifestyle choices and managing chronic health conditions

Practical strategies for making healthy lifestyle choices and managing chronic health conditions

1. **Healthy eating:** Incorporate a balanced and nutritious diet consisting of whole grains, fruits, vegetables, lean protein, and healthy fats. Avoid processed foods, sugary drinks, and excessive amounts of salt.
2. **Regular physical activity:** Aim to get at least 30 minutes of moderate physical activity most days of the week. This can include activities such as walking, cycling, swimming, or any form of exercise that you enjoy and that increases your heart rate.
3. **Stress management:** Practice stress-reducing techniques such as meditation, deep breathing, yoga, or progressive muscle relaxation. Identify the sources of stress in your life and work on ways to manage or eliminate them.
4. **Sleep hygiene:** Establish a consistent sleep routine and aim for 7-9 hours of sleep per night. Avoid screens before bedtime, create a relaxing bedtime routine, and create a sleep-conducive environment.
5. **Tobacco and alcohol cessation:** Quit smoking and limit alcohol consumption to reduce the risk of various chronic health conditions.
6. **Chronic condition management:** If you have a chronic health condition, work closely with your healthcare provider to develop a management plan that includes regular check-ups, medication management, and lifestyle modifications.
7. **Support system:** Surround yourself with friends, family, or support groups who can offer encouragement, motivation, and accountability.
8. **Regular health screenings:** Stay up to date on recommended health screenings for your age and health status, such as mammograms, colonoscopies, and blood pressure checks.
9. **Take Time for Self-Care:** Make time for activities that bring you joy and relaxation, such as reading, taking a bath, or spending time in nature.
10. **Set Realistic Goals:** Set achievable goals for yourself and track your progress. Celebrate your successes, and be kind to yourself if you slip up. Making healthy lifestyle choices is a journey, not a destination.

Remember, making healthy lifestyle choices and managing chronic health conditions requires effort and dedication, but the benefits to your overall health and well-being are worth it.

CHAPTER FOUR

Manifesting Happier Relationships

Discuss the role of our thoughts and beliefs in shaping our relationships

Our thoughts and beliefs play a crucial role in shaping our relationships with others. Our thoughts and beliefs about ourselves, others, and the world around us determine how we communicate, how we perceive and interpret events, and how we respond to different situations.

For example, if someone has a belief that all people are fundamentally good, they are likely to approach their relationships with others with trust and positivity, leading to stronger and more fulfilling connections. On the other hand, if someone has a belief that people are inherently selfish and untrustworthy, they may approach relationships with suspicion and negativity, which can lead to strained or unhealthy relationships.

Similarly, our beliefs about others can also impact our relationships. If we hold negative stereotypes or prejudices about a particular group of people, it can lead to distrust, conflict, and emotional distance in our relationships.

Moreover, our beliefs about what a healthy relationship should look like and how people should treat each other can affect the quality and success of our relationships. For example, if an individual believes that compromise and open communication are essential in a relationship, they are more likely to work on resolving conflicts and improving their relationship.

Here are some affirmations for happier relationships that you can use to attract more love, harmony, and joy into your relationships:

1. *I am surrounded by loving and supportive people who bring joy and happiness into my life.*
2. *I am worthy of love and happiness in my relationships, and I attract loving and supportive partners and friends.*
3. *I am grateful for the relationships in my life, and I cherish the moments of love and joy that we share.*
4. *I am open to receiving and giving love in my relationships, and I allow myself to fully experience the joy of being loved and appreciated.*
5. *I am releasing all negative thoughts and emotions that are hindering my relationships, and I am filling my mind with positive thoughts and emotions that promote love and harmony.*
6. *I am communicating clearly and openly with my partners and friends, and I am cultivating deeper connections and understanding.*
7. *I am embracing the differences in my relationships and celebrating the unique qualities that each person brings.*
8. *I am forgiving and releasing all past hurts and grudges, and I am creating a new foundation of love and trust in my relationships.*
9. *I am taking care of myself and my needs, and I prioritize my own well-being and happiness in my relationships.*
10. *I am creating a life of love and happiness, and I am attracting people and experiences that support this joyful lifestyle.*

Remember to repeat these affirmations daily with a sense of belief and positivity, and visualize yourself already living in happy and fulfilling relationships. By aligning your thoughts and emotions with the frequency of love and joy, you can attract more love and happiness into your relationships and create deeper connections and harmony with greater ease and joy.

In conclusion, our thoughts and beliefs are like filters through which we view and interpret the world. By being aware of and actively working to change negative thoughts and beliefs, we can improve our relationships and create healthier, more fulfilling connections with others.

Tips and techniques for fostering love, compassion, and forgiveness towards oneself and others

What is fostering love:

Fostering love refers to taking steps to nurture and develop love in a relationship or family. It is the process of creating an environment where love can flourish, grow and deepen over time. This can involve taking the time to understand and support each other, practicing empathy and compassion, expressing appreciation and affection, resolving conflicts in a healthy and positive way, and sharing common experiences and interests. Fostering love can help strengthen the bonds between individuals, create a positive and supportive atmosphere, and increase feelings of happiness and well-being.

Fostering love, compassion, and forgiveness towards oneself and others can be a lifelong practice, and it can be challenging, but it is also rewarding. Here are some tips and techniques that might be helpful:

1. **Practice self-compassion:** Treat yourself with the same kindness, care, and understanding that you would offer to a good friend. Speak to yourself with compassion and avoid self-criticism.
2. Cultivate gratitude: Focus on the things you are thankful for, including your own qualities and strengths.
3. **Practice mindfulness:** Pay attention to the present moment without judgment. This can help you better understand and accept your thoughts and emotions.
4. **Forgive yourself:** Everyone makes mistakes. Learn to let go of past failures and negative self-talk.
5. **Exercise empathy:** Try to understand others' perspectives and feelings. This can help you develop compassion and reduce feelings of judgment and anger.
6. **Engage in acts of kindness:** Doing something kind for others can increase positive feelings and promote a sense of connection.
7. **Surround yourself with positive relationships:** Spending time with supportive people who love and accept you for who you are can help you feel better about yourself and foster more positive relationships with others.
8. **Seek support when needed:** Talking to a trusted friend, family member, or therapist can help you process and manage your emotions in a healthy way.
9. **Challenge negative thoughts:** When negative thoughts arise, try to challenge them with more balanced, positive perspectives.

10. **Practice patience and non-judgment:** Be patient with yourself and others. Avoid jumping to conclusions or assuming negative intentions.

Remember, these practices take time and effort, but they can help you develop a more positive and loving outlook on life.

Practical strategies for improving communication, resolving conflicts, and attracting fulfilling relationships

Improving communication

Improving communication is a key factor in building and maintaining strong relationships. Here are some practical strategies for improving communication:

1. **Active Listening:** Pay attention to the speaker, show interest and understanding, and ask questions to clarify. Avoid distractions, interruptions, and making assumptions.
2. **Empathy:** Try to see the situation from the other person's perspective, acknowledge their feelings, and respond with understanding and compassion.
3. **Clear and Honest Communication:** Be direct and clear about your thoughts, feelings, needs, and expectations. Use "I" statements to express yourself and avoid blaming or attacking the other person.
4. **Nonverbal Communication:** Be aware of your body language and tone of voice, as they can convey just as much as the words you say.
5. **Ask Questions:** Encourage open and honest communication by asking questions and expressing interest in what the other person has to say.
6. **Avoid Criticism and Contempt:** Criticism and contempt can quickly erode trust and make it difficult to effectively communicate. Instead, focus on finding common ground and working together to resolve any issues.
7. **Seek Understanding:** Make an effort to understand the other person's point of view, even if you don't agree with it. This can help to reduce misunderstandings and improve the overall quality of communication.

By incorporating these strategies into your interactions with others, you can develop stronger, more effective communication skills and build healthier, more fulfilling relationships.

Practical strategies for resolving conflicts

Conflicts are a natural part of any relationship, but they can be managed and resolved in a healthy and constructive way. Here are some practical strategies for resolving conflicts:

1. Identify the root cause: Try to understand the underlying reasons for the conflict. This can help to address the real issue and find a solution that works for everyone.
2. **Stay calm:** Conflicts can be emotionally charged, but it's important to remain calm and level-headed. Take a break if necessary, and come back to the discussion when you're both ready.
3. **Use "I" statements:** Express your own thoughts, feelings, and concerns, rather than blaming the other person. This can help to defuse the situation and promote understanding.
4. **Listen actively:** Pay attention to the other person, acknowledge their perspective, and avoid interrupting. Try to understand their point of view and show empathy.
5. **Brainstorm solutions together:** Work together to find a mutually-beneficial solution that addresses the root cause of the conflict.
6. **Compromise:** Be willing to give and take. Compromise can be a powerful tool for resolving conflicts and finding common ground.
7. **Follow up:** Make sure to follow up on any agreements made during the conflict resolution process. This can help to ensure that everyone stays on the same page and that the issue doesn't resurface.

By following these strategies, you can effectively manage and resolve conflicts in a way that strengthens your relationships and promotes mutual understanding and respect.

Practical strategies for attracting fulfilling relationships

Attracting fulfilling relationships requires effort and attention to one's own personal growth and well-being, as well as being open to new experiences and connections. Here are some practical strategies for attracting fulfilling relationships:

1. **Work on self-improvement:** Focus on developing a positive self-image, improving communication skills, and increasing self-awareness. This can help you to attract healthy, fulfilling relationships.
2. **Be open-minded:** Be open to meeting new people and trying new experiences. This can help to broaden your social network and increase your chances of making meaningful connections.
3. **Practice self-care:** Taking care of yourself is important for attracting fulfilling relationships. Make sure to prioritize your physical and emotional well-being and maintain a healthy balance between work and play.
4. **Be genuine:** Be yourself, and don't try to be someone you're not. Authenticity and sincerity can attract others who appreciate and value you for who you are.
5. **Maintain a positive attitude:** A positive outlook on life can help to attract people who are supportive, understanding, and appreciative.
6. **Show interest in others:** Ask people about their interests, and listen to what they have to say. Being attentive and caring can help to build rapport and foster meaningful connections.
7. **Set healthy boundaries:** It's important to set clear boundaries in relationships and to respect the boundaries of others. This can help to create a positive and supportive environment for all parties involved.

By implementing these strategies, you can increase your chances of attracting fulfilling relationships that bring joy, fulfillment, and a sense of connectedness into your life.

CHAPTER FIVE

Manifesting Your Dreams

The importance of having a clear vision and purpose in life

What is Clear Vision?

A clear vision is a clear and vivid understanding of where you want to go in life and what you want to achieve. It's a future-oriented perspective that provides direction and purpose and helps you to make decisions and set goals that align with your values and aspirations.

A clear vision is not just about having a destination in mind, but also about having a clear understanding of the values, beliefs, and principles that guide you on your journey. It's a way of envisioning the best version of yourself, and the life you want to create.

Having a clear vision can be empowering and can help to bring clarity, focus, and motivation to your life. It can provide a sense of direction, and help you to overcome challenges and setbacks by keeping you focused on your goals and aspirations.

Overall, a clear vision is an essential component of personal growth, achievement, and overall well-being, and is a valuable tool for anyone looking to create a fulfilling and meaningful life.

What is the purpose of life?

Purpose in life refers to the reason for which you exist or the reasons for which you pursue certain goals or activities. It is a sense of meaning and direction that provides a foundation for decision-making, goal-setting, and overall well-being.

Purpose can come from many sources, including personal values, beliefs, spirituality, relationships, and experiences. Some people find their purpose through their careers, while others find it through their relationships, personal growth, or community involvement.

Having a sense of purpose can be a powerful motivator, helping you to persevere through difficult times and to pursue your goals with passion and determination. It can also bring a sense of fulfillment and satisfaction, as you are living a life aligned with your values and beliefs.

Discovering your purpose in life can be a journey of self-discovery, and may take time and introspection. However, the process of discovering your purpose can be a valuable and rewarding experience and can lead to a greater sense of meaning and well-being.

Overall, having a sense of purpose in life is an essential component of personal growth, achievement, and overall well-being, and is a valuable tool for anyone looking to create a fulfilling and meaningful life.

Having a clear vision and purpose in life is essential for personal fulfillment and overall well-being. Here are some of the benefits of having a clear vision and purpose:

1. **Direction:** A clear vision and purpose can provide direction and focus in life, helping you to make decisions and set goals that align with your values and aspirations.
2. **Motivation:** Having a sense of purpose can be a powerful motivator, inspiring you to pursue your passions and work towards a meaningful future.
3. **Improved Mental Health:** A clear vision and purpose can help to reduce stress and anxiety, and increase feelings of happiness, satisfaction, and well-being.
4. **Increased Resilience:** A clear vision and purpose can help you to bounce back from setbacks and challenges, as you have a greater sense of meaning and direction in life.
5. **Better Relationships:** When you have a clear vision and purpose, you are more likely to attract people who share your values and goals, which can lead to stronger and more fulfilling relationships.
6. **Personal Growth:** Having a clear vision and purpose can help you to grow and develop as a person, as you continuously strive towards your goals and aspirations.

7. **Legacy:** A clear vision and purpose can help you to leave a lasting legacy, making a positive impact on the world and leaving a legacy for future generations.

In summary, having a clear vision and purpose can bring clarity, direction, and meaning to life, and can lead to a more fulfilling and satisfying existence. It's never too late to start exploring your purpose and creating a vision for your life.

Tips and techniques for aligning your thoughts and actions with your goals

Here are some tips and techniques that can help you align your thoughts and actions with your goals:

1. **Write down your goals:** Writing down your goals makes them concrete and helps you to keep track of your progress. When you see your goals written down, it's easier to stay motivated and focused on what you want to achieve.
2. **Prioritize your goals:** Make a list of your goals and prioritize them based on their importance to you. This will help you focus on the most important tasks first and allocate your time and energy more effectively.
3. **Break down your goals into smaller, manageable tasks:** Breaking down your goals into smaller, achievable tasks can make them feel less daunting and more achievable. It also allows you to see progress and keep your motivation levels high.
4. **Create a plan of action:** Once you have broken down your goals into smaller tasks, create a plan of action that outlines the steps you need to take to achieve each one. Be specific and include deadlines for each task.
5. **Keep a positive mindset:** Having a positive attitude and outlook will help you stay motivated and focused on your goals. Surround yourself with positive people and try to avoid negativity as much as possible.
6. **Hold yourself accountable:** Make a commitment to yourself to follow through on your goals and hold yourself accountable for your actions. Keep track of your progress and celebrate your successes along the way.
7. **Stay flexible:** Life is unpredictable and sometimes things don't go as planned. Be open to adjusting your goals and plans as needed, but still remain focused on your end goal.

8. **Get support:** Surround yourself with people who support and encourage you. Having a support system can help keep you accountable and motivated when things get tough.

Remember, aligning your thoughts and actions with your goals takes time and effort, but with persistence and determination, you can achieve the success you desire.

Practical strategies for overcoming obstacles and pursuing your passions

Here are some practical strategies for overcoming obstacles and pursuing your passions:

1. **Identify your obstacles:** The first step in overcoming obstacles is to identify what they are. This could be a lack of time, resources, skills, or confidence. Once you know what your obstacles are, you can start to develop a plan to overcome them.
2. **Create a plan of action:** Develop a step-by-step plan that outlines the actions you need to take to overcome your obstacles. Be specific and include deadlines for each step. This will help keep you on track and give you a sense of control.
3. **Stay motivated:** Pursuing your passions can be challenging, but it's important to keep your motivation levels high. Surround yourself with positive people and things that inspire you. Celebrate your successes along the way and remind yourself why your passions are important to you.
4. **Build a support network:** Having a support network of friends, family, or colleagues who believe in you and your passions can help you stay motivated and overcome obstacles. Seek out mentors or join groups of like-minded individuals who can offer guidance and support.
5. **Take action:** The most important step in overcoming obstacles and pursuing your passions is taking action. Don't wait for the perfect moment or the perfect circumstances - start taking small steps toward your goals today.
6. **Learn from failures:** Don't be discouraged by setbacks or failures. Use them as opportunities to learn and grow. Seek feedback, reflect on what went wrong, and identify what you can do differently next time.

7. **Stay persistent:** Overcoming obstacles and pursuing your passions requires persistence and determination. Keep pushing forward, even when things get tough. Remember, success is a journey, not a destination, and the most important thing is to keep moving forward.
8. **Practice self-care:** Taking care of yourself is important for overcoming obstacles and pursuing your passions. Make time for activities that bring you joy and reduce stress, such as exercise, hobbies, or spending time with loved ones.
9. **Practice Gratitude:** Practicing gratitude is a powerful tool that can help you manifest your dreams.

By following these strategies, you can overcome obstacles and pursue your passions with confidence and resilience. Stay focused on your goals, stay motivated, and don't give up!

CHAPTER SIX

Practice the Gratitude - Manifesting Your Dreams

What is Gratitude?

Gratitude is the quality of being thankful and appreciative for the good things in life. It is an attitude of recognizing and acknowledging the positive aspects of one's life, no matter how small or seemingly insignificant. Gratitude involves focusing on what you have rather than what you lack, and cultivating a mindset of abundance and positivity.

Gratitude is not just about saying "***thank you***" when someone does something nice for you. It's about noticing the good things in your life, no matter how small, and feeling genuinely grateful for them. It's about appreciating the people, experiences, and opportunities that come your way and recognizing that they are all gifts.

Gratitude has been shown to have many benefits, both physical and psychological. It can improve mood, reduce stress, enhance relationships, and even boost the immune system. By cultivating a practice of gratitude, you can increase your overall sense of well-being and happiness, and attract more positivity and abundance into your life.

Overall, gratitude is a powerful tool that can help you shift your focus from what you lack to what you already have, and cultivate a mindset of abundance and positivity.

Gratitude is one of the most powerful tools to manifest your dreams because it helps shift your focus from what you lack to what you already have. When you cultivate a mindset of gratitude, you become more aware of the abundance in your life, which in turn attracts more abundance and positive experiences to you.

Here are a few reasons why gratitude is so effective in manifesting your dreams:

1. **Gratitude puts you in a positive mindset:** When you focus on what you're grateful for, you naturally feel more positive and optimistic. This positive mindset attracts more positive experiences into your life, which can help you manifest your dreams.
2. **Gratitude helps you align with the universe:** The law of attraction states that like attracts like. When you focus on gratitude, you align yourself with positive energy and attract more of it into your life.
3. **Gratitude helps you let go of resistance:** Resistance can block the flow of abundance and prevent you from manifesting your dreams. Gratitude helps you release resistance and trust in the universe to provide for you.
4. **Gratitude helps you appreciate the journey:** Manifesting your dreams is not just about achieving a certain goal, it's about enjoying the journey and appreciating the present moment. Gratitude helps you appreciate the progress you've made and the experiences you've had along the way.

Overall, gratitude is a powerful tool because it helps you focus on the positive and cultivate a mindset of abundance. By practicing gratitude regularly, you can shift your energy and attract more of what you want into your life, making it easier to manifest your dreams.

Practicing gratitude is a powerful tool that can help you manifest your dreams.

Here are some steps to practice gratitude and manifest your dreams:

1. **Start your day with gratitude:** When you wake up in the morning, take a moment to appreciate everything in your life that you are grateful for. This can be as simple as saying a prayer of thanks or writing down a few things in a journal.
2. **Focus on what you want:** Instead of focusing on what you don't have or what you're lacking, focus on what you want to manifest in your life. Visualize yourself already having what you want and feel gratitude for it.

3. **Use affirmations:** Affirmations are powerful statements that you can repeat to yourself to reinforce positive beliefs and thoughts. Create affirmations that focus on gratitude for what you want to manifest, such as "I am grateful for the abundance of love and joy in my life."
4. **Express gratitude throughout the day:** Take time throughout your day to express gratitude for the people and things in your life. This can be as simple as saying "thank you" to someone who has helped you or appreciating the beauty of nature.
5. **Keep a gratitude journal:** Write down the things you are grateful for each day in a journal. This can help you focus on the positive and reinforce your gratitude practice.

By practicing gratitude, you are creating a positive mindset and opening yourself up to receiving the things you want in life. Remember to be patient and trust in the process of manifesting your dreams. With time and practice, you can create a life full of joy, abundance, and gratitude.

Here are some gratitude affirmations that you can use to manifest your dreams:

1. *I am grateful for all the abundance in my life, and I attract even more abundance every day.*
2. *I am grateful for my dreams, and I trust that the universe is working to bring them into reality.*
3. *I am grateful for the opportunities that come my way, and I am open to receiving even more opportunities.*
4. *I am grateful for the love and support of those around me, and I attract even more love and support into my life.*
5. *I am grateful for my health and well-being, and I take good care of my mind, body, and spirit.*
6. *I am grateful for the challenges that have helped me grow, and I trust that I can overcome any obstacle that comes my way.*
7. *I am grateful for the beauty in the world around me, and I appreciate the little things that bring me joy every day.*
8. *I am grateful for my talents and abilities, and I use them to make a positive impact on the world.*

9. *I am grateful for the abundance of opportunities that come my way, and I trust that the universe is guiding me toward my highest good.*
10. *I am grateful for the present moment, and I embrace every moment with joy, gratitude, and positivity.*

Remember to repeat these affirmations regularly and truly believe in them for them to be most effective in manifesting your dreams. By cultivating a gratitude mindset, you can attract more positivity and abundance into your life, and manifest your dreams with ease.

CHAPTER SEVEN

Real Life Success Stories

Here are some real-life examples of relationship manifestation success stories:

1. ***Finding a soulmate:***

    a. Sarah had been single for many years and was starting to feel like she would never find a partner. She started practicing manifestation techniques and created a list of qualities that she wanted in a partner. She visualized herself in a happy and loving relationship, feeling grateful and joyful every day. One day, she met John, who had all the qualities on her list and more. They fell in love and are now happily married.

    b. Samantha was single and feeling lonely. She decided to focus on manifesting a loving relationship with a partner who shared her values and interests. She began visualizing herself in a happy relationship and repeating positive affirmations about attracting love into her life. One day, she met a man at a coffee shop who shared her passion for hiking and outdoor adventures. They hit it off immediately and began dating. Now, Samantha is in a happy and fulfilling relationship with her soulmate, whom she attracted through her positive thoughts and intentions.

2.

Healing a relationship:

a. David and his father had a strained relationship for many years. They rarely spoke and when they did, it was usually filled with tension and conflict. David started practicing manifestation techniques and visualized himself and his father having a loving and peaceful relationship. He also started expressing his love and appreciation for his father more often, despite the past conflicts. Over time, their relationship improved and they were able to communicate more openly and lovingly. They now have a strong and loving relationship.

b. Jack and Lilly had been married for several years, but their relationship had become stagnant and unfulfilling. They decided to try manifesting a happier and more loving relationship by focusing on the positive aspects of their marriage and visualizing themselves in a happy and loving partnership. They also began communicating more openly and honestly with each other, expressing their needs and desires. Over time, their relationship transformed, and they rediscovered their love and passion for each other. They are now happier and more fulfilled in their marriage than ever before.

3.

Attracting more love and happiness:

a. Sri Mitra was feeling stuck in her relationships and wanted to attract more love and happiness into her life. She started practicing manifestation techniques and focused on visualizing herself surrounded by love and joy every day. She also started expressing gratitude for the love that was already present in her life. Over time, she attracted more positive and loving people into her life and her relationships became more fulfilling and joyful.

b. Jennifer had just gone through a painful breakup and was feeling hopeless about finding love again. She decided to use manifestation techniques to attract a new relationship into her life. She began focusing on positive affirmations about finding true love and visualizing herself in a happy relationship. She also worked on releasing any negative beliefs or emotions that were holding her back. A few months later, she met a man who shared her interests and values. They began dating and fell deeply in love. Jennifer is now in a happy and loving relationship with the man of her dreams, whom she attracted through her positive thoughts and intentions.

Here are a few real-life examples of money manifestation success stories:

1. Jack Canfield, the co-author of the popular book series "Chicken Soup for the Soul," once shared how he manifested a $100,000 check. He wrote the amount on a piece of paper and placed it on his ceiling so he would see it every morning and night. Within a year, he received a check for exactly $100,000 from a book publisher.
2. Actress Jim Carrey once wrote himself a check for $10 million for "acting services rendered," dated it for five years in the future, and carried it in his wallet as a reminder of his goal. Before the five years were up, he had earned $10 million for his role in the movie "Dumb and Dumber."
3. Entrepreneur and author Marie Forleo often talk about how she used visualization and affirmation techniques to manifest a successful career and financial abundance. She would visualize herself achieving her goals and repeat affirmations like "I am abundant" and "I am capable of creating financial freedom."
4. In her book "The Secret," author Rhonda Byrne shares numerous success stories of people who have used the law of attraction to manifest money and financial success. One story involves a woman who started visualizing herself receiving unexpected checks in the mail, and within a few weeks, she received a check for $50,000 from an unexpected source.
5. Finally, many people have shared their own personal success stories with money manifestation techniques like vision boards, affirmations, and gratitude journaling. For example, some people have manifested unexpected bonuses at work, new job opportunities with higher salaries, or even winning the lottery.

Here are a few examples of health manifestation success stories:

1. Recovery from cancer: Many people have successfully used manifestation techniques to overcome cancer. One example is Anita Moorjani, who was diagnosed with stage 4 cancer and was given just hours to live. However, after having a near-death experience, she came back to life and found that her cancer had completely disappeared. She attributed her recovery to her belief in the power of manifestation and positive thinking.
2. Overcoming chronic pain: Another example is the story of Dr. Joe Dispenza, who suffered a severe spinal injury in a cycling accident that left him with chronic pain. After traditional medical treatments failed to alleviate his pain, he turned to meditation and visualization techniques to heal his body. Through his practice, he was able to fully heal his injury and overcome his chronic pain.
3. Weight loss: Many people have used manifestation techniques to achieve their weight loss goals. One such example is the story of Sarah Prout, who struggled with her weight for years before discovering the power of manifestation. By focusing on positive affirmations and visualizing herself at her ideal weight, she was able to lose over 40 pounds and keep it off.
4. Healing from depression: Depression is a complex and challenging condition to overcome, but many people have found success by using manifestation techniques to shift their mindset and overcome negative thought patterns. One example is the story of Marie Forleo, who battled depression for years before discovering the power of gratitude and positive affirmations. Through her practice, she was able to overcome her depression and create a happy, fulfilling life for herself.

These are just a few examples of the many ways in which manifestation techniques can be used to improve our health and well-being. While they may not work for everyone, they are certainly worth exploring for those who are seeking to improve their physical, emotional, or spiritual health.

CHAPTER EIGHT

Summery

This self-help book "**Manifesting Your Best Life** "provides valuable insights into the Law of Attraction and how to manifest specific things in your life, such as financial abundance, better health, and happier relationships.

Here are some key takeaways from the book:

1. The Law of Attraction is always working: The Law of Attraction is based on the principle that like attracts like. This means that your thoughts and emotions create your reality, and you attract into your life whatever you focus on.
2. Focus on what you want: To manifest specific things in your life, it's important to focus on what you want, rather than what you don't want. This means visualizing and feeling the emotions associated with having what you desire.
3. Take inspired action: While it's important to focus on positive thoughts and emotions, you also need to take inspired action towards your goals. This means taking small steps towards your desires and trusting that the universe will guide you towards the right path.
4. Gratitude and positivity attract abundance: Gratitude and positivity are powerful tools for manifesting abundance in your life. By focusing on the good things in your life and feeling grateful for them, you attract more positive experiences and abundance.
5. Believe in yourself and your ability to manifest: Believing in yourself and your ability to manifest your desires is key to the Law of Attraction. This means letting go of limiting beliefs and trusting that you have the power to create the life you want.

Overall, This Book is a valuable resource for anyone looking to manifest specific things in their life. By focusing on what you want, taking inspired action, cultivating gratitude and positivity, and believing in yourself, you can attract financial abundance, better health, happier relationships, and anything else you desire. So if you're ready to continue your journey of manifestation, this book is definitely worth a read.

The importance of persistence, patience, and self-reflection in the manifestation process

Manifestation is a powerful process that involves attracting what we desire into our lives through our thoughts and actions. It's a practice that requires patience, persistence, and self-reflection. In this article, we'll explore the importance of these three qualities in the manifestation process and how they can help us achieve our goals.

Persistence

Persistence is the act of continuing to work towards a goal, even when faced with challenges and setbacks. In the manifestation process, persistence is key. It's important to remain focused on our desires and continue taking action toward them, even when things don't go as planned.

For example, if we're trying to manifest a new job, we may experience rejection or setbacks during the job search process. But if we remain persistent and continue to apply for jobs and network with potential employers, we increase our chances of manifesting the job we desire.

Patience

Patience is the ability to remain calm and composed while waiting for something to happen. In the manifestation process, patience is crucial. It's important to trust that the universe will bring our desires to us at the right time, even if it doesn't happen as quickly as we'd like.

For example, if we're trying to manifest a romantic relationship, we may feel impatient and frustrated if we don't meet someone right away. But if we remain patient and continue to focus on our desires, we increase our chances of meeting the right person when the time is right.

Self-Reflection

Self-reflection is the process of examining our thoughts, emotions, and actions to gain a deeper understanding of ourselves. In the manifestation process, self-reflection is important because it helps us identify any limiting beliefs or negative thought patterns that may be blocking our desires.

For example, if we're trying to manifest financial abundance, but we have a deep-seated belief that money is evil or that we don't deserve wealth, we may unintentionally sabotage our manifestation efforts. By engaging in self-reflection and identifying these limiting beliefs, we can work to overcome them and create a more positive mindset toward our desires.

In conclusion, the manifestation process requires persistence, patience, and self-reflection. By remaining persistent in our efforts, trusting in the timing of the universe, and examining our thoughts and beliefs, we can overcome obstacles and achieve our goals. So, let us embrace these qualities and continue on our journey toward manifestation.

Do you ever feel like life is just happening to you? That you have no control over the things that happen in your life? It's easy to fall into the trap of thinking that we are powerless to change our circumstances, but the truth is, we have the power to create our own reality.

You see, everything in our lives is a manifestation of our thoughts, beliefs, and actions. If we want to live the life of our dreams, we have to first believe that it's possible and then take action to make it happen.

How do we embrace our power to create our reality and live the life of our dreams?

Here are a few steps to get started:

1. Identify your desires: The first step in creating your reality is to identify what you truly desire. This can be anything from a fulfilling career to a loving relationship to financial abundance. Take some time to really think about what you want and write it down.
2. Visualize your desires: Once you've identified your desires, the next step is to visualize them as if they have already come true. Close your eyes and imagine yourself living the life of your dreams. What does it look like? How does it feel?
3. Believe in yourself: The key to creating your reality is to believe that it's possible. Believe in yourself and your ability to make your dreams a reality. Let go of any limiting beliefs that are holding you back.

4. Take action: Visualization and belief are important, but they're not enough on their own. You have to take action toward your desires. This might mean taking small steps toward your goal every day or making a big leap of faith. Whatever it is, take action toward your dreams.
5. Trust the process: Creating your reality is not always easy, and there will be times when things don't go as planned. But it's important to trust the process and have faith that everything is working out for your highest good.

In conclusion, you have the power to create your own reality and live the life of your dreams. By identifying your desires, visualizing them, believing in yourself, taking action, and trusting the process, you can make your dreams a reality. So, embrace your power and start living the life you truly desire.

With Love And Gratitude

Thank you for reading "**Manifesting Your Best Life.**" I hope that this book has been a valuable resource for you on your journey to create a life of purpose, joy, and abundance.

As you continue on your path, I invite you to stay connected with me and the community of like-minded individuals who share your passion for personal growth and transformation. Here are some ways you can stay connected:

Visit my Youtube channel **https://www.youtube.com/@umanilakantam** for resources, tools, and updates on upcoming events and workshops.

Follow me on social media for daily inspiration and guidance.

Instagram: https://www.instagram.com/umanilakantam

Twitter: https://twitter.com/umanilakantam

Facebook: https://www.facebook.com/umanilakantam

And finally, I would be grateful if you could take a moment to leave a review of this book on your favorite retailer or book review site. Your feedback helps me improve and grow, and it also helps others discover the book.

Thank you again for your support, and ***I wish you all the best*** on your journey to manifesting your best life.

With love and gratitude,

Uma Nilakatam

9 798889 864219

Printed by Libri Plureos GmbH in Hamburg,
Germany